KU-197-268

LS 0750 **221178** 8003

Leabharlanna Atha Cliath
SCHOOLS LIBRARY
Invoice : 99/3479 Price IR£12.27
Title: Family from Japan
Class:

FAMILIES AROUND THE WORLD

A family from
JAPAN

Simon Scoones

WAYLAND

FAMILIES AROUND THE WORLD

A family from **BOSNIA**

A family from **GUATEMALA**

A family from **BRAZIL**

A family from **IRAQ**

A family from **CHINA**

A family from **JAPAN**

A family from **ETHIOPIA**

A family from **SOUTH AFRICA**

A family from **GERMANY**

A family from **VIETNAM**

The family featured in this book is an average Japanese family. The Ukitas were chosen because they were typical of the majority of Japanese families in terms of income, housing, number of children and lifestyle.

Cover: The Ukita family outside their home with all their possessions.
Title page: Sayo hangs out the family's washing.
Contents page: Children run down the street in the local shopping area.

Series editor: Katie Orchard
Designer: Tim Mayer
Production controller: Carol Titchener

Picture Acknowledgements: All the photographs in this book were taken by Peter Menzel. The photographs were supplied by Material World/Impact Photos and were first published by Sierra Club Books in 1994 © Copyright Peter Menzel/Material World.
The map artwork on page 4 is produced by Peter Bull.

First published in 1997 by Wayland Publishers Limited
61 Western Road, Hove
East Sussex, BN3 1JD, England

© Copyright 1997 Wayland Publishers Limited

Find Wayland on the Internet at http://www.wayland.co.uk

Typeset by Mayer Media
Printed and bound by G. Canale & C.S.p.A., Italy

British Library Cataloguing in Publication Data

Scoones, Simon
    A family from Japan. – (Families around the world)
    1. Family – Japan – Juvenile literature
    2. Japan – Social life and customs – Juvenile literature
    I. Title
    306.8'5'0952

ISBN 0 7502 2117 8

Contents

● Introduction

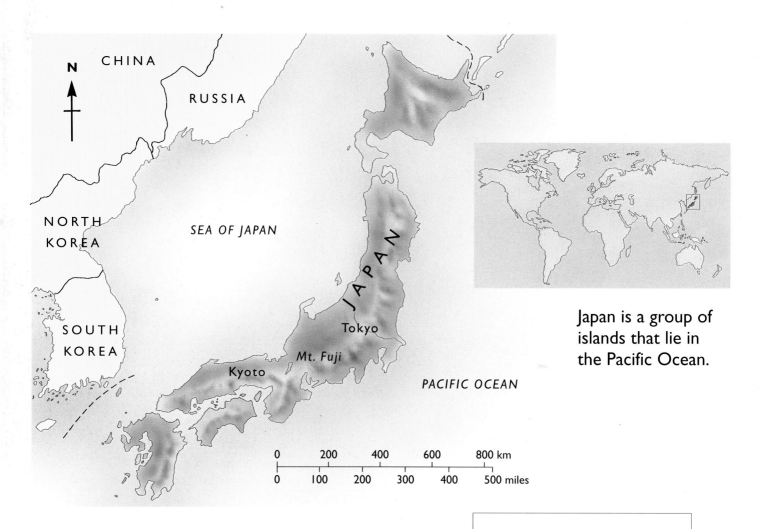

CHINA

RUSSIA

N

NORTH
KOREA

SEA OF JAPAN

SOUTH
KOREA

J A P A N

Tokyo

Mt. Fuji

Kyoto

PACIFIC OCEAN

0   200   400   600   800 km

0   100   200   300   400   500 miles

Japan is a group of
islands that lie in
the Pacific Ocean.

JAPAN	
Capital city:	Tokyo
Size:	377,997 square kilometres
Number of people:	125,900,000
Language:	Japanese
People:	Mostly Japanese, some Korean and Chinese
Religion:	Shinto, Buddhist, Confucianist, Christian
Currency:	Yen

THE UKITA FAMILY

Size of household:	4 people
Size of home:	132 square metres
Work week:	Kazuo: 40 hours
	Sayo: 60 hours (at home)
Most valued possessions:	Kazuo: Grandmother's ring
	Sayo: Grandfather's pottery
	Mio: Her unicycle
	Maya: Her dog, Izamaru
Family income:	US$26,824

The Ukita family is an average Japanese family. The Ukitas have put everything that they own outside their house so that this photograph could be taken.

Meet the family

EARTHQUAKE!

Japanese people have learned to live with the danger of earthquakes. Long ago, people believed that earthquakes happened when a giant catfish shook its tail in the ocean.

1 Kazuo, father, 45
2 Sayo, mother, 43

3 Mio, daughter, 9
4 Maya, daughter, 6

The Ukita family live in a small, two-storey house on the edge of Tokyo, Japan's largest city. They only have to walk five minutes to reach Mio and Maya's grandparents' house. There is not much space in Tokyo, so houses are built close together. The Ukita family don't have a garden of their own, but there is a park close by.

'We have a normal-sized family for Japan today, but in the old days, families were much bigger. My mother had seven children including me.' *Sayo*.

The Ukita house

The Ukita family's house has two storeys. The bedrooms and bathroom are upstairs, and the kitchen and living room are downstairs.

CROWDED CITIES

Mountains cover most of Japan, so most Japanese people live on the flatter land along the coast. To make new pieces of land, engineers drain off water from the sea. In the cities, some roads are built on top of buildings because there is not enough room on the ground.

A Home of Their Own

Houses are expensive in Japan so the Ukita family are lucky to own their home. The house is quite small with five rooms, but it is modern and has everything that the family needs. The Ukita family owns another house in the countryside. Every few months, the Ukitas drive to their other house to enjoy the fresh air and open space.

The Latest Technology

The television in the living room has the latest technology. The remote control has a special button so that the family can listen to a programme in either Japanese or English. Mio and Maya like to watch cartoons on television. Kazuo prefers to watch the sports programmes.

Before bedtime, Mio likes to relax in front of the television with a cold drink.

Keeping Warm

Like many families in Japan, the Ukita family do not have heating in their house. When it is cold in the winter they have an extra pile of blankets to cover themselves and keep warm.

Bedrooms

Mio and her sister share a room and they have bunk beds. Kazuo and Sayo sleep on a futon in their bedroom. A futon is a traditional type of bed that is made out of planks of wood and then covered with a mattress.

Mio's bedroom is the best place for peace and quiet. This is where she does her homework.

'We always take off our shoes before we go indoors. It shows respect for a person's home, and it also keeps the place clean!' *Mio*.

Food and cooking

The Ukitas have a lot of machines to make life easier. Sayo finds the microwave oven very useful.

A CAREFUL COOK

Japanese food is very different from food in other countries, but it is becoming popular all over the world. One very expensive dish is cooked *fugu*, which is a pufferfish. The cook has to be very careful – eating the wrong part of the fish can kill you.

Choosing the Ingredients

Sayo is an excellent cook, and she takes a lot of care to make sure the family is well fed. Luckily, Sayo has plenty of shops nearby so she can spend time looking for the ingredients that she needs. The supermarket has plenty of choice, with food from all over the world. But Sayo usually buys fresh vegetables from the local shop where they are cheaper.

Breakfast

In the morning, Sayo prepares toast and coffee for the whole family. Sayo always makes sure the children eat breakfast before they go to school.

◀ Sayo pops into the supermarket for some last-minute dinner ingredients.

Sayo is proud of her kitchen. She always keeps it spotlessly clean.

Lunch Time

Mio and Maya have lunch at school with their classmates. Some Japanese food is quite unusual. Mio's favourite snack is a grasshopper, cooked in soy sauce and sugar. It's delicious!

Manners

The girls know that it is important to have good table manners. Sticking your chopsticks upright in your rice is very rude in Japan.

Mio and her school friends have their lunch in one of the classrooms.

Family Supper

The evening meal is a good time for the family to sit down together and share the day's news. Before eating, the family says, '*itadakimasu*' to thank the people who produced the food. Sayo believes that it is important to arrange the food beautifully on each plate. She likes to make *sushimi*, which is raw fish on top of a bed of rice. Kazuo likes to eat his *sushimi* with *wasabi*. This is a spicy sauce made of herbs, horseradish and soy sauce.

Sometimes the Ukitas like to watch television while they're eating.

Working hard

MODERN TECHNOLOGY

Japanese companies are world-famous for making the latest designs in cars and electronics. Japanese televisions, stereos, cameras, cars and kitchen equipment are sold all over the world.

Kazuo has several suits. He likes to look smart at work.

Kazuo works for a company that sells foreign books to shops. He is always very busy checking that the right books have arrived. Kazuo likes to make sure that all his customers are happy.

Kazuo's brother is a special kind of doctor called an acupuncturist. He treats illnesses by pricking his patients' skin with needles. Acupuncture is an ancient kind of Chinese medicine.

Kazuo catches up on the news on his way to work.

Getting to Work

Kazuo's job is in the middle of Tokyo so he has to travel to work by train. The journey takes an hour and a half, and he has to change trains twice.

'The trains always run exactly on time. I usually reach the platform about a minute before my train arrives!' *Kazuo*.

> 'We don't have space to dry clothes indoors, so I use a special pole to hang my washing out on the balcony. The wind does the rest of the work.' *Sayo*.

Working at Home

Sayo is very busy at home. She gets up half an hour before everyone else to make the family's breakfast. Sayo takes a lot of care to make sure that the house is clean and tidy. At the end of the year, Mio and Maya help their mum to clean every corner of the house. This gives their home a fresh start for the new year to come.

Down to the Shops

Sayo goes to the local shops twice a week to buy food for the family. Sometimes she bumps into her friends while she's shopping and stops for a chat. On the way home, Sayo finds it difficult to carry lots of bags of shopping, especially during hot weather.

Sayo hoovers the floor while the rest of the family are out of the way.

School life

Mio gets lots of homework. She likes to have all her books near her desk.

STUDYING HARD

A school day in Japan starts at half-past-eight in the morning and ends at half-past-four in the afternoon. Children have to go to school on Saturdays. Many children take extra lessons in the evenings and on Saturday afternoons to help them pass exams.

Every morning, Sayo walks with Maya and Mio to their school to make sure that they get there safely. Each school day is seven hours long, although there are breaks during the day.

Maya and Mio both love sport. They really enjoy PE lessons when they can play games such as volleyball, and play on the ropes and jumps in the gym. During breaktime, Mio likes to skip over a rope while her friends sing and clap.

'Before school, I like to meet up with my friend, Akiko. Today, we're playing with her new camera.' *Maya.*

Passing Tests

Mio has to work very hard so that she can pass the examinations to get into a good junior high school next year. To improve her chances, Mio spends some time every evening doing her homework. On Saturday mornings, she attends '*juku*', where she has extra lessons in the subjects that she finds more difficult.

Mio's teacher puts the best work of the class on the classroom walls.

Mio also enjoys her lessons in Japanese dance. She is practising hard for a school show at the end of the year.

'I'm glad I don't have exams yet. My sister always has to work really hard.' *Maya.*

Starting School

Maya does not have to worry about examinations yet. She has only just started to go to school. Maya enjoys learning how to count and how to write the difficult Japanese alphabet.

Leisure and play

Maya often practises playing the family piano.

HOLIDAYS

Many Japanese families spend their spare time in the mountains. There are beautiful waterfalls and the famous volcano, Mount Fuji. In the winter, there is enough snow for people to be able to ski. Japan also has its own Disneyland.

Getting Away

During the long school holiday in the summer, the Ukitas sometimes go abroad to learn about different countries. The family has already visited Europe and Hawaii. One day, Sayo hopes to go to the USA to visit an old school friend.

'I walk our dog in the park near our house. His name is Izamaru, and he is nearly as big as me!' *Maya.*

At the Weekend

The Ukita family is often busy at the weekends.
Mio swims in the local swimming-pool on Sunday
mornings. She practises for two hours with
100 other children. Maya is learning how to play
the piano and she has lessons on Saturdays.

Mio wears goggles when
she is swimming. They stop
the water from stinging
her eyes.

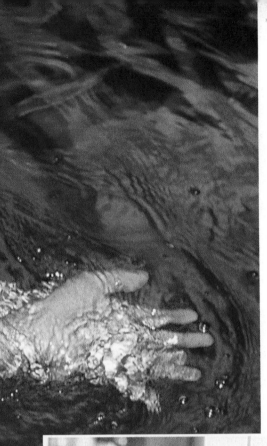

Meeting Friends

Kazuo likes to rest on Sundays, but sometimes he goes to a *karaoke* club with his friends. He enjoys singing along to his favourite songs, even though he sings completely out of tune!

▼ Kazuo enjoys a night out at a *karaoke* club.

The future

Mio and her mum have fun when they go shopping.

A Change for Women

Mio and Maya both want to do well at school so that they will be able to have good jobs when they grow up. Already, more women in Japan are choosing to have fewer children and have jobs as well. The girls already have plans for their careers. Mio wants to be a doctor when she grows up and Maya wants to be a famous musician.

School is finished for the day, so these children run off to play.

Timeline

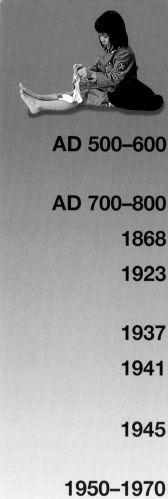

AD 500–600	Buddhism comes from China and Korea, and introduces the Chinese style of writing to Japan.
AD 700–800	The Emperor of Japan makes Kyoto its capital.
1868	Tokyo becomes Japan's new capital city.
1923	The Kanto earthquake hits Tokyo and kills over 142,000 people.
1937	Japan invades the Chinese province of Manchuria.
1941	The USA and Japan enter the Second World War. Japan attacks US forces at Pearl Harbor, Hawaii.
1945	US forces drop atomic bombs on the Japanese cities of Hiroshima and Nagasaki, ending the Second World War.
1950–1970	The Japanese rebuild their country to make it one of the most successful in the world.
1995	An earthquake in the city of Kobe kills 5,250 people.

Glossary

Atomic bombs Very powerful bombs that destroy a huge area.

Buddhism A religion followed by millions of people, mainly in Asia.

Chopsticks Made from wood, plastic or metal, chopsticks are used for eating food instead of knives and forks.

Earthquakes A violent shaking of the Earth's surface. Earthquakes can cause a lot of damage to people and buildings.

Electronics Modern machines that need electricity.

Emperor A ruler of a large area of land called an empire.

Engineers People who build roads, bridges and buildings.

Juku Extra school lessons that happen at the weekends.

Karaoke A popular pastime in Japan, where people sing along to their favourite tunes.

Noodles Strips or rings of pasta, usually made with egg.

Province An area of a country.

Pufferfish A fish that can puff itself up to look like a spiky football.

Volcano A mountain, usually cone-shaped, with a crater. Molten rock and hot ashes can be thrown out of the crater.

Volleyball A team game where the players push a ball over a net with their hands.

Further information:

Books to read:

Japan, Country Insights series, by Nick Bornoff (Wayland, 1996)

Japan by Dr Bryan Coates (Wayland, 1991)

Passport to Japan by Richard Tames (Watts, 1993)

Organizations:

Japan Information and Cultural Centre, Japanese Embassy, 101–104 Piccadilly, London W1V OAH.

Index